SCHOLASTIC

W9-BHZ-105

Grades K-2

TIC-TAC-MATH

50 Reproducible, Leveled Game Sheets That Kids Can Use Independently or in Small Groups to Practice Important Math Skills

by Sue Hansen

NEW YORK • TORONTO • LONDON • AUCKLAND • SYDNEY
MEXICO CITY • NEW DELHI • HONG KONG • BUENOS AIRES

Teaching *Resources*

*This book is dedicated to my marvelous family,
my magnificent friends, and my colleagues and co-workers
who encouraged me to put my creative ideas into a book.
Thanks for your support, laughter, and love
for playing games while learning.*

Scholastic Inc. grants teachers permission to photocopy the designated reproducible pages from this book for classroom use. No other part of this publication may be reproduced in whole or in part, or stored in a retrieval system, or transmitted in any form or by any means, electronic, mechanical, photocopying, recording, or otherwise, without written permission of the publisher. For information regarding permission, write to Scholastic Inc., 557 Broadway, New York, NY 10012.

Cover design by Jaime Lucero
Interior design by Grafica
Illustrations by Maxie Chambliss

ISBN 0-439-62919-5

Copyright © 2005 by Sue Hansen
All rights reserved.
Printed in the U.S.A.

1 2 3 4 5 6 7 8 9 10   40   12 11 10 09 08 07 06 05

Table of Contents

Introduction

Welcome to *Tic-Tac-Math: Grades K–2!* Your students are about to experience a wonderfully educational twist on one of the most popular games of all time. After all, what better way to grab children's interest than to announce, "Today, we're going to play a game!"

Just like classic tic-tac-toe, *Tic-Tac-Math* is played on a three-by-three grid that children mark with X's and O's to make a win. But unlike the traditional game, each square in the grid contains a math problem that children have to solve correctly before they can claim the square with their X or O.

What's Inside

Inside this book, you'll find 50 *Tic-Tac-Math* grids. Each grid covers a specific math skill that is tied to at least one of the NCTM (National Council for Teachers of Mathematics) standards. There are five sections that address the main standards: Number & Operations, Algebra, Geometry, Measurement, and Data Analysis & Probability. (See page 7 for a brief overview of each math standard to give you an idea of the types of problems and activities in each *Tic-Tac-Math* grid.) A special section offers fun mathematical challenges where children guess mystery numbers, work with a hundred chart, and practice calendar skills. You'll also find a blank grid on page 8—make photocopies of this grid to use as answer sheets for children or to create your own Tic-Tac-Math problems.

Within each section, the *Tic-Tac-Math* grids increase in difficulty, challenging children to a higher level of mathematical thinking and problem solving. You can use this book to differentiate your instruction and meet the needs of all learners with different mathematical abilities, whether it's a child who needs practice with a specific math skill or a child who is ready to extend his or her learning with higher-level thinking skills. By the time children have completed every grid in this book, they will have reviewed most of the major math skills covered from kindergarten through 2nd grade.

How to Use This Book

Tic-Tac-Math is a great way to reinforce a current math lesson or review a topic. Simply photocopy the page that corresponds with your unit of study and distribute to children.

Children can play *Tic-Tac-Math* with a partner, in small groups, or individually. Partners can play following the conventional rules of the game. Consider these additional rules as well:

- Flip a coin to decide who goes first, and who will be X and who will be O.

- If a player solves a problem correctly, that player marks the space with his or her letter (X or O).

- If the player answers incorrectly, the other player gets to mark that space with his or her letter *unless* that space would give the first player Tic-Tac-Math. (Players must correctly complete three problems in a row horizontally, vertically, or diagonally to get Tic-Tac-Math.)

- To win, a player must successfully solve the problem on the winning game space.

- Remind players to check each other's work!

Here are a few more ideas for using *Tic-Tac-Math:*

- **As a daily warm-up:** Have children complete one of the problems as a warm-up at the start of the class. Challenging children with a quick math problem when they first enter the classroom helps them get settled and ready to work.

- **To reinforce a lesson:** After teaching a math lesson, hand out a *Tic-Tac-Math* grid for practice and reinforcement.

- **For "fast finishers":** Make sure to have some grids to give children as a "What to Do When You're Done" activity.

- **For homework:** Send home a sheet for children to practice a particular skill with parents or siblings. You may want to copy the simple directions on page 5 that explain how the game works.

- **As a center or choice activity:** Offer Tic-Tac-Math as a fun activity for center or choice time. Consider copying the grids onto cardstock and even laminating them so you can reuse them. Children can use different-colored counters instead of marking the grids with their X's and O's. Store the grids in a labeled folder or envelope for easy access. If you are using several different grids during one game session, encourage children to rotate around the room and play with as many other children as possible. Children gain a great deal from learning how to work with those to whom they might not normally gravitate toward in class.

Whichever approach you decide to use, your students are sure to enjoy themselves as they build the skills they need to succeed in math and on standardized tests. Let the games begin!

Meeting the NCTM Standards

The different sections of *Tic-Tac-Math: Grades K–2* correlate with the NCTM standards. Here's an overview of each standard:

Number and Operations The Number and Operations content standard should be at the center of mathematical learning in the primary grades. In Grades K–2, children should be involved in many mathematical activities that deal with numbers and making sense of numbers, such as counting, numeral recognition, place value, number relationships, and solving numeric story problems. Also included in this math standard are numeric operations like addition and subtraction. Multiplication (grouping objects in multiples) and division (sharing things equally) should also be introduced in the primary grades but at a level that meets young children's abilities. Encourage children to share their strategies for solving any numeric problems.

Algebra From the most basic skills of sorting and classifying to the challenge of solving missing-number problems using variables, algebra can be taught at the primary grades. At the core of the Algebra content standard is patterns. Learning about repeating patterns and growing patterns and how to translate patterns will be vital to children developing other algebraic skills and concepts. Other concepts include skip counting, ordering objects (and ordering numbers), numeric relations, functions, equality, commutative property, and qualitative relationships. Show children how to use pictures, objects, or symbols to help them understand these algebraic concepts. Encourage them to use various strategies to help them solve algebraic problems.

Geometry Under the Geometry content standard, we teach K–2 students about 2-dimensional shapes (such as circles, squares, and hexagons) and 3-dimensional shapes (such as cubes, pyramids, and cones). We want children to see that geometric shapes are all around us—in doors, windows, gumballs, buildings, and more! Children should be able to name, recognize, draw, build, and compare both 2-D and 3-D shapes. Geometry also includes spatial relations and visualization concepts. Spatial skills lead into the idea of relative position (above, behind, near) and positional words (up, down, over, in, out). Students should learn to read maps, use coordinates, follow paths, and determine distance, location, and direction.

Measurement The Measurement content standard includes more than simply measuring with a ruler or tape measure. The measurement content standard covers time, money, length, weight, capacity, temperature changes, calendar skills, fractions, ordering objects, and even estimation. There should be a lot of hands-on learning within the measurement standard for the K–2 student. Children should be using nonstandard measurement tools (such as paper clips, interlocking cubes, and shoes) in kindergarten and the early part of first grade. In late first grade and throughout second grade, children should begin using standard measurement tools (such as rulers, tape measures, weights, and scales) in addition to nonstandard tools.

Data Analysis and Probability The Data Analysis and Probability content standard may seem like a 'hefty' concept for K–2 students, but this standard focuses student learning on asking questions, gathering data, organizing data, formulating answers, and reporting information. All of these skills should relate to the child's world (for example, find out how many kids wear shoes that tie or how many pets does each child have.) To report the data, children will begin to use tally sheets, charts, bar graphs, and other types of graphs. Ask children questions such as how much, how many, what kind, which of these, and more. The other part of this content standard deals with probability. At the K–2 level probability should be taught very informally. Focus on likely/unlikely events and fair/unfair activities that would occur in the children's world. Playing games with spinners and dice are a great way to practice these concepts with children.

Name(s): _____

Name(s): _____

What's My Number?

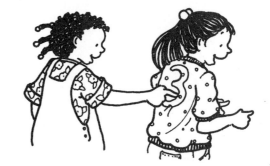

Answer three problems to get
Tic-Tac-Math!

Fill in the missing numbers.

1 _____ 3 4 _____

6 7 _____ 9 _____

Count:

• from 7 to 17.

• from 2 to 20.

• from 10 to 19.

• from 5 to 25.

• from 3 to 23.

Circle all the number ones that you see.

41	10	100	16
5	17	52	101
	91	6	

Write the number that comes after each number below.

2 _____   10 _____

4 _____   16 _____

Ask a friend to trace a number on your back using her finger. Try to guess the number. Do this several times.

What number has been left out of each row?

1	2	4	5	6	7

3	4	5	6	8	9

10	9	7	6	5	4

How many fingers do you have?

_____ fingers

How many toes do you have?

_____ toes

Write the numbers from zero to 10 in the spaces below.

_____ _____ _____

_____ _____ _____

_____ _____ _____

_____ _____

Circle the larger number.

7 or 17   ⋮   9 or 4

12 or 2   ⋮   1 or 5

3 or 7   ⋮   8 or 0

Scholastic • Tic-Tac-Math: Grades K–2

Name(s): _____

Number Sense

Answer three problems to get Tic-Tac-Math!

Count to:

- 8 but begin at 2.
- 9 but begin at 3.
- 12 but begin at 5.
- 10 but begin at 4.
- 20 but begin at 11.

Circle the smaller number.

4 or 10	9 or 3
2 or 5	11 or 15
9 or 1	8 or 7

Fill in the missing numbers.

5 _____ 7

8 _____ 10

11 _____ 13

13 _____ 15

Can you skip count by 5's? On the back of this sheet, write the numbers you say, starting with 5.

Write the numbers from 4 to 12 in the spaces below.

_____ _____ _____

_____ _____ _____

_____ _____ _____

Count backward:

- from 10 to 0.
- from 8 to 2.
- from 15 to 5.
- from 20 to 10.
- from 26 to 12.

Write the number next to each word.

one _____

six _____

three _____

four _____

Circle all of the 5's you see below.

96	15	55
4	5	105
525	65	17

How many "teen" numbers can you write?

_____ _____ _____

_____ _____ _____

_____

Scholastic • *Tic-Tac-Math: Grades K–2*

Name(s): _____

Getting to Know Numbers

Answer three problems to get Tic-Tac-Math!

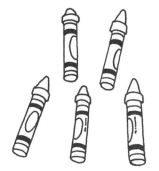

Write the number next to each word.	**Solve the addition problems.**	**Write the number that comes before each number below.**
two _____ ten _____ nine _____ nineteen _____	1 + 0 = _____ 2 + 0 = _____ 3 + 0 = _____ 4 + 0 = _____	_____ 7 _____ 2 _____ 13 _____ 10
You have 5 crayons. If you give away 2 of your crayons, how many crayons will you have left? _____ crayons	**Fill in the missing numbers.** 5 _____ 7 _____ 9 10 _____ 12 _____ _____ 15 _____ 17 18 _____ 20	**On the back of this paper, draw these animals in this order.** • The cat is first. • The fish is second. • The dog is third.
Write four numbers that end with a zero. _____ _____ _____ _____	**Count backward by 1's. Write the numbers.** 17 16 _____ _____ _____ _____ _____	**Can you skip count by 10's? Count to someone from 10 to 100. Then skip count by 10's backward from 100 to 0.**

Scholastic • Tic-Tac-Math: Grades K–2

Name(s): _____

Numbers Everywhere!

Answer three problems to get Tic-Tac-Math!

Count the dots on each square. Write the number under the square.

_____   _____

Fill in the missing numbers.

_____ 13 _____ 15 16

17 _____ 19 _____ 21

_____ 23 _____ _____

Use tally marks to show each number.

2 _____

4 _____

7 _____

Solve the addition problems.

6 + 1 = _____

7 + 1 = _____

8 + 1 = _____

9 + 1 = _____

Draw a line to match the number to the number word.

3   six

6   seven

7   two

2   three

What is:

- 1 less than 5? _____
- 1 less than 7? _____
- 1 less than 10? _____
- 1 less than 19? _____
- 1 less than 1? _____

All of the numbers below are alike except for one. Circle the number that is not like the others.

20   80   10   100

30   25   50   90

Look in your kitchen for numbers. Draw pictures on the back of this paper to show where you found numbers in your kitchen.

Write five numbers that are greater than 15.

_____ _____ _____

_____ _____

Scholastic • Tic-Tac-Math: Grades K–2

Name(s): _____

Missing Numbers

Answer three problems to get Tic-Tac-Math!

Write six numbers that are greater than 25.

_____ _____ _____

_____ _____ _____

Count by 10's. Write the numbers.

8 18 _____ _____ 48

_____ _____ 78 _____

Subtract.

6 – 0 = _____

5 – 0 = _____

4 – 0 = _____

3 – 0 = _____

Here are 4 squares:

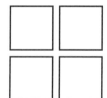

Is the number odd or even? _____

Can you skip count by 2's? Write the numbers you say below.

2 4 _____ _____

_____ _____ _____

_____ _____ _____

Fill in the numbers that come before and after each number.

_____ 12 _____

_____ 20 _____

_____ 7 _____

_____ 36 _____

Add.

1 + 1 = _____

2 + 2 = _____

3 + 3 = _____

4 + 4 = _____

Subtract.

6 – 1 = _____

5 – 1 = _____

4 – 1 = _____

3 – 1 = _____

In each row, circle the number that doesn't belong.

1	2	3	27
22	33	98	55
45	10	30	90

Name(s): _____

Writing Numbers

Answer three problems to get Tic-Tac-Math!

Make tally marks for:	Circle the smaller number.	What is:
25 _____	51 or 15 21 or 20	• 10 plus 2 more? _____
29 _____		• 10 plus 4 more? _____
18 _____	98 or 88 17 or 71	• 10 plus 6 more? _____
		• 10 plus 8 more? _____

Subtract.

$10 - 9 =$ _____
$10 - 8 =$ _____
$10 - 7 =$ _____
$10 - 6 =$ _____
$10 - 5 =$ _____

Fill in the missing numbers.

10 ____ 30 ____ ____

60 ____ ____ 90 ____

110 ____ 130 ____

Solve the problems.

$1 + 2 + 3 =$ _____
$4 + 2 + 2 =$ _____
$3 + 3 + 2 =$ _____
$4 + 1 + 1 =$ _____

Are the answers odd or even? _____

Count by 10's.

4   14 ____ ____

44 ____ 64 ____

____ 94 104 ____

On the back of this paper, write all of the ways you know how to make five. Use tallies, pictures, equations, drawings, and so on.

Write six even numbers that you know.

____ ____ ____

____ ____ ____

Scholastic • Tic-Tac-Math: Grades K–2

Name(s): _____

Making Sense of Numbers

Answer three problems to get Tic-Tac-Math!

Fill in the blanks with numbers that will make each equation true.

_____ + _____ = 10

_____ + _____ = 10

_____ + _____ = 10

Circle all the odd numbers.

7   12   20   5   39

81   16   87   40   23

Fill in the missing numbers.

99 _____ 101 102

_____ 104 _____ 106

_____ 108 _____ 110

Which number is different from the others? Circle it.

331   336   303

332   339   337

Write the number next to each word.

fifty-three _____

eighty-eight _____

one hundred five _____

seventy-two _____

Fill in the blanks with numbers that will make each equation true.

_____ − _____ = 0

_____ − _____ = 0

_____ − _____ = 0

_____ − _____ = 0

Solve. Watch the signs!

5 + 1 = _____

6 − 0 = _____

2 + 4 = _____

3 + 3 = _____

7 − 1 = _____

Fill in the box with <, >, or =.

5 ☐ 9

16 ☐ 12

2 + 2 ☐ 4

100 ☐ 102

Count backward by 2's starting at 19. Write the numbers you say.

19 17 _____ _____ _____

_____ _____ _____

15

Scholastic • Tic-Tac-Math: Grades K–2

Name(s): _____

I've Got Your Number!

Answer three problems to get Tic-Tac-Math!

Fill in the missing numbers.

424 _____ 426 _____

_____ _____ 430

_____ 432 _____

On the back of this paper, draw these colors in the order listed.

- A red line first
- A yellow line last
- A blue line second
- A green line third

This is a doubles fact:

$2 + 2 = 4$

Write three more doubles facts.

What is:

- 10 more than 6? _____
- 10 more than 59? _____
- 10 more than 210? _____
- 10 more than 629? _____

This domino shows 9.

Make three more dominoes that show 9.

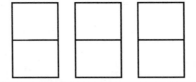

Write some odd numbers.

_____ _____ _____ _____

_____ _____ _____ _____

Circle the largest number you wrote.

Solve.

$15 - 5 =$ _____

$14 - 4 =$ _____

$13 - 3 =$ _____

$12 - 2 =$ _____

$11 - 1 =$ _____

Fill in the missing numbers.

$2 +$ _____ $= 10$

_____ $+ 7 = 9$

$4 +$ _____ $= 8$

_____ $+ 2 = 7$

	7	
1		3

Use these numbers to make:

- the smallest 3-digit number. _____
- the largest 3-digit number. _____

Scholastic • Tic-Tac-Math: Grades K–2

Name(s): _____

Numbers Get Bigger

Answer three problems to get Tic-Tac-Math!

Write the number that is 10 more than each number word.

fifty-two _____

thirty-three _____

one hundred eight _____

two thousand ten _____

Solve.

5 + 4 = _____

15 + 4 = _____

15 + 4 + 5 = _____

15 + 4 + 5 + 10 = _____

Count backward by 2's, starting at 29. Can you get to zero?

yes   no

What does the 4 represent in the number 749?

_____

Follow these steps to get to a number:
- Start with 2.
- Add 4.
- Add 20.
- Subtract 6.

What number did you get? _____

Write four facts that equal 20.

_____ + _____ = 20

_____ + _____ = 20

_____ + _____ = 20

_____ + _____ = 20

Write the number that is 100 more than:

226 _____

439 _____

72 _____

150 _____

Solve.

3,826 + 1 = _____

3,826 + 10 = _____

3,826 + 100 = _____

3,826 + 1,000 = _____

Fill in the missing number that will make each equation true.

10 − _____ = 8

15 = _____ + 7

100 = 1 + _____

16 − 6 = _____

Name(s): _____

What's in a Number?

Answer three problems to get Tic-Tac-Math!

Read the clues to figure out the mystery number.

- 2 groups of 5
- 1 less than 11
- 8 + 2

The mystery number is

_____ .

Color in $\frac{1}{2}$ of the square.

Sarah needs 12 straws for a science project. She has 5. How many more straws does she need?

Color $\frac{3}{5}$.

Color $\frac{1}{2}$.

Circle the number that has 8 in the hundreds place.

68	481
872	8,405

How many eyes do three people have in all? Show your answer on the faces below.

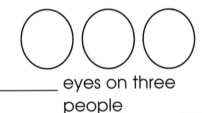

_____ eyes on three people

Circle each group of 3 below. How many groups of 3 did you make?

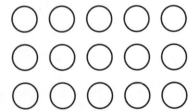

What is 1,000 more than:

562? _____

85? _____

3,920? _____

1,471? _____

Solve.

10 + 5 = _____

200 + 40 + 6 = _____

5,000 + 900 + 30 + 2 = _____

900 + 8 = _____

Name(s): _____

Hurray for Patterns!

Answer three problems to get Tic-Tac-Math!

Finish these patterns.

x o x o x o _____ _____

A B A B _____ _____

1 2 1 2 1 2 _____ _____

O o O o _____ _____

Use 2 different colors to make a striped pattern.

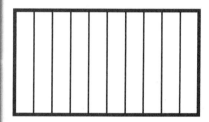

Create your own snap–clap pattern. Have a friend listen to your pattern. Can he or she copy it? Ask your friend to make his or her own snap–clap pattern for you to copy.

How old are you?

_____ years old

How old will you be next year?

_____ years old

Color a pattern.

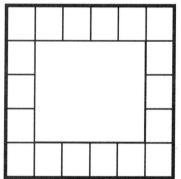

Finish the pattern.

○ ▢ ○ ▢

___ ___ ___ ___

On the back of this paper, create your own pattern using three different colors. Label your pattern.

Write three places where you see patterns at home or at school.

_____

_____

_____

Write four numbers and four letters in this chart.

Numbers	Letters

Name(s): _____

Do You See a Pattern?

Answer three problems to get Tic-Tac-Math!

Find five toys. Line them up from smallest to largest. Find five more toys. Can you fit them in the line so all the toys still go from smallest to largest? Show two people what you did.

For each color below, write something that comes in that color.

red _____

blue _____

yellow _____

Finish these letter patterns.

A B C A B C _____ _____

X Y Z X Y _____ _____

H I J H I J _____ _____

Add.

$5 + 1 =$ _____

$6 + 1 =$ _____

$7 + 1 =$ _____

What pattern do you see with the answers?

Use two colors to create a checkerboard pattern.

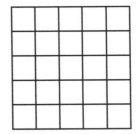

Draw objects to match each number.

7	9

Finish these number patterns:

1 2 1 2 1 _____ _____

1 2 3 1 2 _____ _____

1 1 2 1 1 _____ _____

1 2 2 1 2 _____ _____

Solve.

OO
OO + OO =

O
O + OOO
OOO =

Make a striped, 3-color pattern on this T-shirt.

Scholastic • Tic-Tac-Math: Grades K–2

Name(s): _____

There's a Pattern Here!

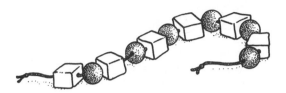

Answer three problems to get Tic-Tac-Math!

Count by 10's starting at 0. What is the fifth number that you say?

_____

Would you ever say 95?

yes   no

Take a small handful of coins. Sort them by the type of coin. Then sort them by another way; for example, by size, date on the coin, and so on.

On the back of this paper, create a 3-color pattern. Leave some blank lines at the end of the pattern. Ask a friend to complete the pattern by filling in the colors on the blank lines.

Finish these patterns.

x X x X x ____ ____

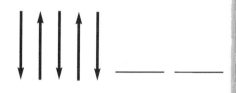

oo O oo ____ ____

Color a pattern on the beaded string.

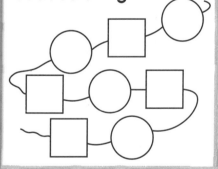

This summer Kim measured 40 inches tall. When school started in the fall, she was 43 inches tall.

How many inches did Kim grow?

_____ inches

Are the following equations true?

1 + 1 = 2   yes no

1 + 1 = 1   yes no

1 + 1 = two   yes no

o + o = oo   yes no

Finish this growing pattern.

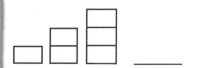

By how much did each block tower grow?

_____

Use three colors to make a pattern.

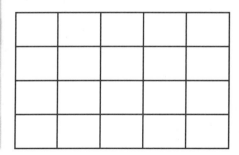

Name(s): _____

Pretty Patterns!

Answer three problems to get Tic-Tac-Math!

Color a pattern.

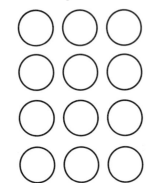

Tasha has a kitten that weighs 5 pounds. When the kitten grows up to be a cat, how much could it weigh?

2 pounds

10 pounds

5 pounds

Are these equations equal?

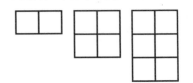

2 + 2 = 4   yes   no

2 + 2 = five   yes   no

2 + 2 = IIII   yes   no

2 + 2 = 4 + 0 yes   no

2 + 2 = four   yes   no

Finish these patterns.

2 4 6   _____ _____

3 6 9   _____ _____

1 3 5   _____ _____

10 9 8   _____ _____

Finish this pattern of counting by 10's.

9 19 29   _____ _____

_____ _____ _____

Draw what comes next.

Finish this pattern.

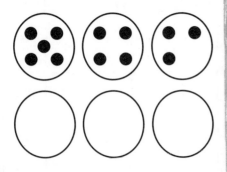

Turn this ABC pattern into a sound pattern. Show a friend the sound pattern you created.

A B C A B C A B C A B C

On the back of this paper, create a four-color pattern. Have someone continue the pattern. Check to see if he or she did it correctly. Label your pattern.

Scholastic • Tic-Tac-Math: Grades K–2

Name(s): _____

Growing Patterns

Answer three problems to get Tic-Tac-Math!

Finish this pattern.

x I x II x III

x _____ x _____

x _____ x _____

x _____

Use four colors to create a pattern in the grid below.

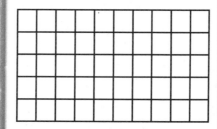

Circle all the equations that are correct.

1 + 1 = 1

2 + 2 = 4

2 + 1 = 3

1 + 2 = 3

3 + 3 = 3

Jose is 7 years old. His brother is 9 years old.

Who is older, Jose or his brother? _____

How many years older?
_____

Draw what comes next in this growing pattern.

oo

oooo

oooooo

oooooooo

Finish the number patterns.

12 14 16 _____ _____

5 15 25 _____ _____

80 90 100 _____ _____

101 202 303 _____ _____

If you count by 10's starting at 23, what number comes after 23?

_____

If you keep on counting this way, would you ever say 73? _____

Fill in the rest of the numbers on this strip.

100
200
300

On the back of this paper, create the pattern below using colors.

A B B C A B B C A B B C

Name(s): _____

Patterns to Bark About!

Answer three problems to get Tic-Tac-Math!

If you saw three dogs in the park, how many legs would there be?

_____ legs

Fill in the chart with combinations of numbers that equal 10.

5	5
4	
	7
2	
1	
	10

If you count by 2's starting at 53, what will the next number be?

_____

Is this number odd or even?

_____

If you wrote all the numbers from 1 to 99 on a piece of paper, how many times would you write zero?

_____

Circle each equation that is true.

$4 + 1 = 1 + 4$

$2 + 2 = 2 + 3$

$1 + 3 = 3 + 1$

$5 + 0 = 4 + 1$

What number comes next?

5	7
50	70
500	700
5,000	7,000

_____   _____

Finish these number patterns.

4   8   12   ____   ____

5   10   15   ____   ____

99   97   95   ____   ____

11   22   33   ____   ____

If you count by 3's starting at 0, what is the first even number you'll say?

Each circle is worth 2 points. How many points for all the circles below?

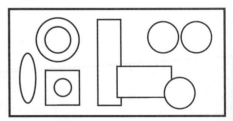

Scholastic • Tic-Tac-Math: Grades K–2

Name(s): _____

Pick a Pattern

Answer three problems to get Tic-Tac-Math!

Finish this pattern.

x

xxx

xxxxx

xxxxxxx

_____

Finish these number patterns.

1 5 9 _____ _____

7 17 27 _____ _____

10 13 16 _____ _____

1 2 4 8 _____ _____

Find an old calendar that you can color on.

• Color the odd numbers red.

• Color the even numbers blue.

What kind of pattern did you color?

Fill in the blank to make each equation true.

8 + _____ = 15

_____ + 9 = 25

17 + 18 = _____

_____ + 25 = 45

If you saw 3 birds in a tree, how many legs would there be?

_____ legs

Read the clues to figure out the mystery number.

• 3 groups of 6

• 1 ten and 8 ones

• 2 less than 20

• one dozen plus 6

The mystery number is

_____ .

Are the equations equal?

5 + 2 = 8 − 1   yes no

10 − 1 = 3 + 3   yes no

9 − 2 = 9 + 2   yes no

10 + 1 = 3 + 7   yes no

One goldfish at the pet store costs 20 cents. How much do 4 goldfish cost?

_____ cents

Sue is 5 years old. Kelsey is 3 years older than Sue.

How old is Kelsey?

_____ years old

How old will Kelsey be in 10 years?

_____ years old

Scholastic • Tic-Tac-Math: Grades K–2

Name(s): _____

Patterns Are Us!

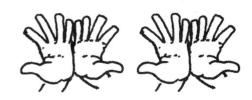

Answer three problems to get Tic-Tac-Math!

On the back of this paper, create an ABCD shape pattern. Make sure your pattern repeats several times. Label your pattern.

Read the clues to figure out the mystery number.

- 50 + 50
- 1 more than 99
- 10 x 10
- 1 less than 101

The mystery number is

_____ .

How many fingers does one person have?

_____ fingers

How many fingers would 6 people have?

_____ fingers

Count by 10's starting at 36. Write the next three numbers you say.

_____ _____ _____

Would you ever say 99?

yes   no

Fill in the blanks to make the equations true.

$10 + 1 = 5 +$ _____

_____ $+ 6 = 2 + 10$

$99 +$ _____ $= 50 + 50$

$25 + 15 =$ _____ $+ 20$

If one toy car costs 50 cents, then 2 toy cars would cost $1.00.

How much would 5 toy cars cost?

_____

Fill in the chart. Use numbers greater than 100.

Odd Numbers	Even Numbers

Fill in the blanks.

1 week = 7 days

2 weeks = 14 days

3 weeks = _____ days

4 weeks = _____ days

5 weeks = _____ days

If you wrote all the numbers from 1 to 100 on a piece of paper, how many times would you write the number one?

_____

Scholastic • Tic-Tac-Math: Grades K–2

Name(s): _____

Finding Shapes!

Answer three problems to get Tic-Tac-Math!

Color all the rectangles green. 	**Write three things that are shaped like a circle.** _____ _____ _____	**Draw a shape that has no straight sides. What is your shape called?**
Guess the shape: • It has four corners. • It has straight sides. • All the sides are the same length. The shape is a _____ .	**Draw a square.** **Draw a rectangle.** How are they alike? How are they different?	**Draw a row of three circles. Under that, draw a row of three squares.**
Find five small toys or objects. Put them on a table. Cover your eyes and have someone take away one of the objects. Can you figure out which object was taken away? Play this several times.	**Color all the squares.** 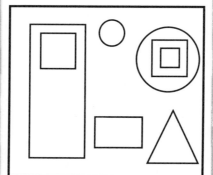	**How many sides on a:** triangle? _____ rectangle? _____ hexagon? _____ square? _____

Scholastic • Tic-Tac-Math: Grades K–2

Name(s): _____

What's in a Shape?

Answer three problems to get Tic-Tac-Math!

Show two different ways to cut a circle in half.

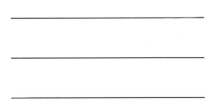

How many squares are in this drawing?

Draw a small circle. Draw a square under the circle. Draw a triangle above the circle.

Write three things that are shaped like a rectangle.

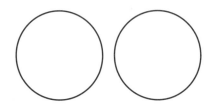

_____

_____

_____

Draw a line to cut each letter in half. Make sure both sides of the letters look exactly the same.

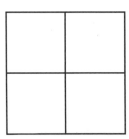

A   T   E

Color all the circles red.

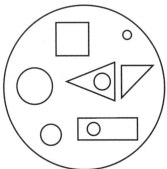

What shape is a:

CD?   _____

postcard?   _____

pizza slice? _____

Divide each rectangle in half. There are four different ways.

Can you name the shapes in this picture?

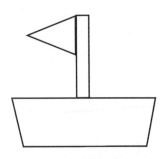

Name(s): _____

Geometry

Answer three problems to get Tic-Tac-Math!

Draw 2 circles and 4 squares.

How many corners on a:

square? _____

triangle? _____

rectangle? _____

circle? _____

Color all triangles red.

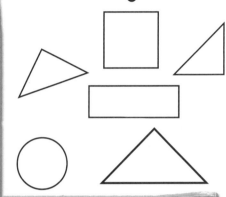

Color all squares blue.

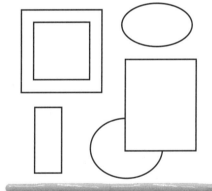

Follow these directions on the back of this paper.

- Draw a big square.
- Draw 4 circles inside the square.
- Draw 2 triangles inside each circle.

Guess the shape:

- It has straight sides.
- It has less than 4 corners.
- It starts with a *t*.

The shape is a

_____ .

Draw a circle.

Draw an oval.

How are they alike?
How are they different?

Have someone draw a shape on your back using their finger. Can you guess what shape they drew? Do this several times.

Trace over the lines to get to the center circle.

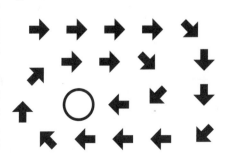

Name(s): _____

The Shape of Things

Answer three problems to get Tic-Tac-Math!

This is a cube.

Find five things that are shaped like a cube.

Color the shapes that are not triangles.

Name the shape that has no corners, no straight sides, and only curved sides.

_____

What is below the triangle?

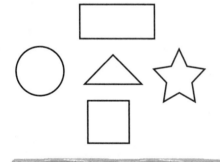

Follow these directions on the back of this paper.

- Draw a big red circle.
- Draw a blue circle inside the red circle.
- Draw a yellow square inside the blue circle.

Use a green crayon to trace the up arrows. Use a blue crayon to trace the down arrows.

How is a square like a cube? List two ways.

_____

_____

_____

_____

Try your best to draw a stop sign. It has eight sides that are the same length. It has eight corners, too.

Draw the missing half of each shape.

Name(s): _____

Shape Up!

Answer three problems to get Tic-Tac-Math!

Copy the dots.

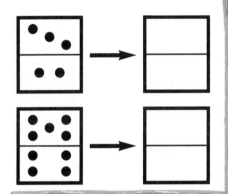

This is a cylinder:

Name two things shaped like a cylinder.

_____

_____

Draw a line to show how you could cut the triangle into two equal parts.

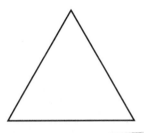

I have three sides and three corners. What shape am I?

_____

Fold a square piece of paper in half. Cut a butterfly shape out of the paper. Color the butterfly so the design and coloring is the same on both sides. This shows symmetry.

Which shapes are not circles?

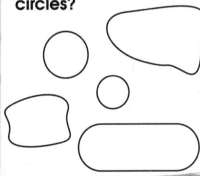

How many squares?

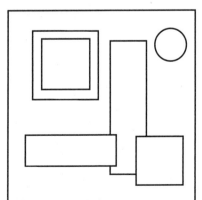

Play a game of tic-tac-toe below.

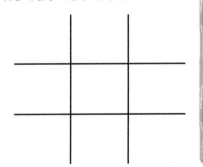

Use four toothpicks to build a square.

• Can you make a rectangle with four toothpicks?

• Can you make a triangle with four toothpicks?

Scholastic • Tic-Tac-Math: Grades K–2

Name(s): _____

Amazing Shapes!

Answer three problems to get Tic-Tac-Math!

Can you name these 3-D shapes?

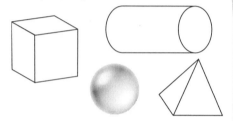

Circle the ones that can roll.

List four things that are shaped like a sphere.

_____

_____

_____

_____

On the back of this paper, create an AABC pattern. Use a circle, a triangle, and a square to make your pattern. Label your pattern and show it to a friend.

Read the clues. Then answer the question.

• Red is on the bottom.

• Yellow is in the middle.

• Blue is the third color.

Where is blue?

_____

Divide each square in half. There are four different ways to do this.

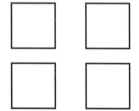

Fold a piece of white paper four or five times. Cut out some small shapes on the folds. Open up the paper. You have a snowflake!

Draw dots on each side of the dice for the numbers 1 to 6. Try to remember the exact position of the dots.

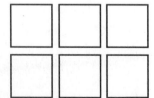

On a piece of paper, follow these directions:

• Draw grass at the bottom.

• Draw a tree on the right.

• Draw a sun above the tree.

• Draw three birds flying under the sun.

How are a sphere and a circle the same? List two ways.

_____

_____

_____

_____

Name(s): _____

Put It Together

Answer three problems to get Tic-Tac-Math!

Connect the dots to make a 5-pointed star.

Use an empty cereal box to make a puzzle. Cut off the front of the box so you have a flat piece. Cut this piece into 7 to 10 smaller pieces. Can you put this puzzle back together?

Which shape below is not a polygon?

Draw the other side of the shape so it is symmetrical.

What shape is a:

gumball? _____

can of soup? _____

box of tissues? _____

Read the clues. Then answer the question.

• Blue is on the top.

• Red is between yellow and blue.

Where is yellow?

_____

A hexagon has six sides and six corners. How many corners are there on six hexagons? Draw a picture to help you solve this problem.

On the back of this paper, draw a line that divides the paper in half the long way. On one side of the paper, draw three 2-D shapes. On the other side, draw three 3-D shapes.

Guess the shape:

• It has corners.

• It has edges.

• It has triangular faces.

• It has a square base.

The shape is a

_____ .

Name(s): _____

Not Just Shapes!

Answer three problems to get Tic-Tac-Math!

How many squares are in this drawing?

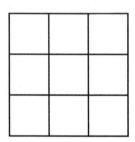

Circle the shape that is the flip of 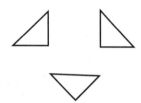.

Color the shapes that are not quadrilaterals.

Which letter looks exactly the same after it has been flipped?

M Z F N

Read the clues. Then answer the question.

• Red is to the right of green.
• Yellow is to the left of green.

Which color is in the middle? _____

This is a rectangular prism:

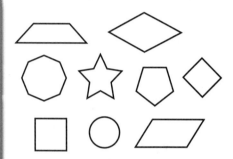

Find five things that are shaped like a rectangular prism.

How many sides on:

4 triangles? _____

3 squares? _____

2 hexagons? _____

Start at the circle. Go right 2 blocks. Go down 2 blocks. Turn left and go 2 blocks. Finally go up 2 blocks. What shape did you make?

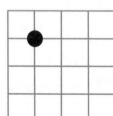

Draw a shape that has 5 corners and 5 sides.

What is your shape called?

_____

Scholastic • Tic-Tac-Math: Grades K–2

Name(s): _____

Time for Measurement

Answer three problems to get Tic-Tac-Math!

If you have 5 pennies, how much money do you have?

_____ cents

If you have 10 pennies, how much money do you have?

_____ cents

Which is heavier? Circle the correct answer.

elephant or mouse

bike or car

feather or brick

skateboard or bike

cat or worm

Write three things in the room that are taller than you.

_____

_____

_____

How many times can you clap in 15 seconds?

_____

Have someone else clap for 15 seconds. How many times did he or she clap?

_____

Fill in the missing numbers on the clock.

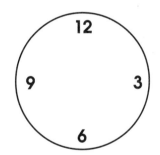

I am thinking of a coin.

- It is silver.
- It has a face on the front.
- It is worth 5 cents.

What is the name of the coin?

_____

What time does school start?

_____

What time does school end?

_____

When do you eat breakfast?

morning   afternoon
night

When do you go to bed?

morning   afternoon
night

How much money is here?

_____ cents

35

Name(s): _____

Weigh It!

Answer three problems
to get Tic-Tac-Math!

Collect some coins and put them on a table. Sort the coins according to their value.

Write one thing that you always do in the morning.

_____

Write one thing that you always do in the afternoon.

_____

Which weighs less? Circle the correct answer.

crayon or shoe

house or bike

mouse or TV

car or telephone

pencil or person

What time do you:

eat dinner? _____

wake up? _____

go to
bed? _____

go to
school? _____

Make a chain using 5 paper clips. Look for things in the room that are about the same length as your chain.

If you have 7 dimes, how much money do you have?

_____

How much is
10 cents more?

_____

Fill in the missing numbers on the clock.

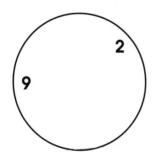

I am thinking of a coin.

• It is silver.

• It has a face on it.

• It is small and thin.

• It is worth ten cents.

What is the name of the coin?

_____

Write the names of the months that end with -ber.

_____

_____

_____

_____

Scholastic • Tic-Tac-Math: Grades K–2

Name(s): _____

Money and More

Answer three problems
to get Tic-Tac-Math!

**Which is worth more?
Circle the correct answer.**

1 dollar or 10 pennies

2 dimes or 1 quarter

10 pennies or 1 nickel

2 nickels or 12 pennies

**On the back of this
paper, write the
names of the months
that have 31 days.**

How much money is here?

_____ cents

**Write three things in the
room that are shorter
than you.**

_____

_____

_____

**Color the longest line
red.**

**Color the shortest line
blue.**

—————— ————

—————————————

————————

——————————

**Write the names of the
days that start with the
letter S.**

_____

_____

_____

**Ask a friend to time you.
How many seconds
does it takes you to:**

• count to 25? _____

• count to 50? _____

• count to 100? _____

**What time is on the
clock?**

_____

**If today is Tuesday,
what day will it be
in three days?**

_____

What day was yesterday?

_____

37

Name(s): _____

Measure These!

Answer three problems to get Tic-Tac-Math!

How much is:

5 pennies? _____ ¢

5 nickels? _____ ¢

5 dimes? _____ ¢

5 quarters? $ _____

Which holds more? Circle the correct answer.

3 cups or 1 cup

1 cup or $\frac{1}{2}$ cup

$\frac{1}{2}$ cup or $\frac{1}{2}$ teaspoon

1 teaspoon or 1 cup

Kendall has 2 quarters and 3 pennies. Jack has 5 dimes and 7 pennies. Who has more?

Kendall   Jack

How old are you?

_____ years old

How old will you be in 2 years?

_____ years old

A small bird might weigh about…

3 inches

3 pounds

50 pounds

Today is Monday, November 3. What will the day and date be in one week?

_____

Show 8:15 on the clock.

What time will it be in one hour?

_____

Show two different ways to make 36 cents.

(Do not use 36 pennies.)

Stretch your fingers wide. From your thumb to your pinkie is one hand length. How many hand lengths is your desk?

_____

Name(s): _____

What's There to Measure?

Answer three problems
to get Tic-Tac-Math!

My cat eats 2 cans of cat food each day. How many cans of cat food does my cat eat in one week?

_____

The temperature this morning was 48 degrees. At noon, it was 69 degrees. How many degrees warmer did it get from morning to noon?

_____

Hook 10 paper clips together. List three things in the room that are as long as the paper-clip chain.

_____

_____

_____

What time is it now?

_____ : _____

What time will it be in 30 minutes?

_____ : _____

How much will it cost to buy the candy and the ice cream?

5¢   25¢

_____¢

Show 3:30 on the clock.

What time was it an hour ago?

_____

Today is Tuesday, December 6. On what day is December 19?

_____

Fill in the missing numbers.

4 quarts = 1 gallon

_____ quarts = 2 gallons

_____ quarts = 3 gallons

2 quarts = _____ gallon

10 pennies = _____¢

10 nickels = _____¢

10 dimes = $_____

10 quarters = $_____

10 one-dollar bills = $_____

39

Name(s): _____

Measure Up!

Answer three problems
to get Tic-Tac-Math!

Which is more? Circle the correct answer.

3 dimes or 2 quarters

4 nickels or 4 dimes

100 pennies or 2 dollars

3 quarters or 8 dimes

7 nickels or 3 dimes

This is a perfect square.

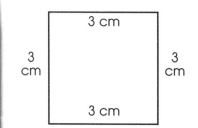

What is its
perimeter? _____ cm

What tool would you use to measure:

• **the length of a pet lizard?**

a ruler   a scale   a cup

• **the weight of a small cat?**

a ruler   a scale   a cup

• **flour to bake cookies?**

a ruler   a scale   a cup

The time now is 11:25. Draw hands on the clock to show the time in half an hour.

In the space below, show 72¢ using the fewest coins possible.

Use a ruler to measure things. List three items that are about 6 inches long.

_____

_____

_____

The temperature outdoors is 93°F. Is it summer or winter?

_____

How much money is shown?

$100	$100	$1
$100	$100	$1
$100	$100	
$100		

$_____

---

one foot = 12 inches

two feet = _____ inches

one yard = 3 feet

one yard = _____ inches

$\frac{1}{2}$ foot = _____ inches

40

Name(s): _____

Fun With Measurement

Answer three problems to get Tic-Tac-Math!

Sam bought 4 movie tickets. Each ticket cost $5.50. How much did the tickets cost in all?

$ _____

Count how many times your heart beats in 10 seconds. Record it here.

_____

How many times would it beat in 1 minute?

_____

The temperature at 8:00 A.M. was 42 degrees. Every hour the temperature went up by 5 degrees.

What will the temperature be at 12:00 noon?

_____

In 5 years, Don will be 19 years old. How old is Don now?

_____ years old

Kim has two cats that each weigh 5 pounds.

She has one dog that weighs 29 pounds.

How much do all her pets weigh together?

_____ pounds

One candy bar costs 50 cents. How many candy bars can you buy for $3.00?

_____ candy bars

A toy helicopter costs 85 cents. If you pay the clerk with 4 quarters, how much change will you get?

_____ cents

Which is longer? Circle the correct answer.

60 seconds or 2 minutes

1 hour or 45 minutes

2 hours or 250 minutes

60 minutes or 600 seconds

Look at the measurements on the triangle.

What is its perimeter?

_____ cm

5 cm   5 cm

3 cm

Measure for Measure

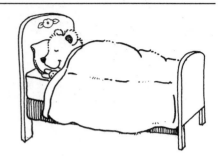

Answer three problems to get Tic-Tac-Math!

I have one quarter and five other coins. Together, they are worth 50¢. What are the five other coins?

_____

What unit would you use to measure:

a pencil?

inches   feet   miles

the length of your room?

inches   feet   miles

Ken gets 10 hours of sleep every night. He goes to sleep at 9:00 P.M.

What time does he wake up in the morning?

_____

---

2 cups   = 1 pint

_____ cups   = 2 pints

2 pints   = 1 quart

_____ cups   = 1 quart

4 quarts   = 1 gallon

_____ quarts = $\frac{1}{2}$ gallon

On the back of this paper, draw a square. Make each side 5 inches long.

What is the square's perimeter?

_____

Ana looked out the window. She saw people wearing jackets, hats, and gloves.

Which is the most likely temperature outside?

70°F   36°F   92°F

This is 1 inch long:

▬▬▬▬▬

Find three things that are about 1 inch long.

Misha's lunch cost $2.45. She paid with a $5 bill.

How much change should she get back?

_____

Hold a book on the palm of your hand. Can you feel how heavy the book is? Find three things that weigh less than the book.

Scholastic • Tic-Tac-Math: Grades K–2

Name(s): _____

Make a Guess

Answer three problems to get Tic-Tac-Math!

On the back of this paper, write the numbers 1 to 20. How many times did you write the number 1?

_____

How many letters are in your first name?

_____

How many letters are in your last name?

_____

Put two different color crayons in a bag. Put your hand in the bag. Make a guess: Which color will you pull out of the bag? Pull out a crayon. Did you guess correctly? Do this a few more times.

Without looking at the calendar, how many Mondays do you think there are in the month?

_____

Now look at the calendar. How many Mondays are there in the month?

_____

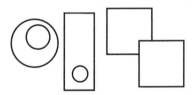

How many:

• circles? _____

• squares? _____

Which is more likely—rain in the summer or snow in the summer?

_____

How many of these things are you wearing?

buttons _____

zippers _____

snaps _____

ties _____

1	2	3	4
0	1	2	3
2	3	4	5
1	2	3	4

How many of each number is in the box?

1 _____   2 _____

3 _____   4 _____

Roll a die (or number cube) ten times. Each time before you roll, guess what number you will roll. How many times did you guess correctly? Use tally marks to keep track.

Name(s): _____

Heads or Tails?

Answer three problems to get Tic-Tac-Math!

Flip a coin ten times. Record how many times heads came up. Do the same for tails.

heads _____

tails _____

How many people live in your house?

_____ people

How many pets live in your house?

_____ pets

2	2	4
1	2	1
4	3	2
1	2	2

How many of each number is in the box?

2 _____   4 _____

1 _____   3 _____

Put 8 red blocks and 4 blue blocks in a bag. Pull one block out of the bag. Make a tally mark next to the color you pulled out. Put the block back in the bag. Repeat 10 times.

red _____

blue _____

On the back of this paper, make a chart. List the names of the boys and girls in your class. Label your chart "Boys" and "Girls."

How many boys' names did you list? _____

How many girls' names did you list? _____

Walk around your house and count how many:

• windows _____

• TVs _____

• beds _____

• sinks _____

Take a look at the tallies you recorded in the box above. Should you have pulled out more red blocks than blue blocks? Explain why you think so.

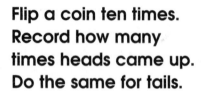

How many circles? _____

How many squares? _____

How many shapes all together? _____

Are there more squares or more circles? _____

Keep track of the morning temperature for a week. Record the temperature below.

Mon.	Tues.	Wed.	Thurs.	Fri.

Which day had the highest temperature? _____

Scholastic • Tic-Tac-Math: Grades K–2

Name(s): _____

Colorful Candies

CHOCOLATE CANDIES	
Red	8
Yellow	12
Blue	5
Orange	3

Answer three problems
to get Tic-Tac-Math!

How many candies are there altogether? _____	Which color has the most candies? _____ Which color has the fewest candies? _____	How many candies are not yellow? _____
Put the number of candies in order from lowest to highest. ____ __ ____ ____	When added together, which two color candies equal 15? _____ _____	How many more orange candies do you need so that the number of orange candies equals red? _____
What is the difference between the number of blue candies and orange candies? _____ – _____ = _____	How many candies are not orange? _____	Which two color candies have a difference of 4? _____ _____ Write an equation to show this.

Name(s): _____

Our Pets

Answer three problems
to get Tic-Tac-Math!

PETS WE HAVE FROM OUR CLASS							
Birds	X	X					
Cats	X	X	X	X	X		
Dogs	X	X	X	X	X	X	X
Fish	X	X	X	X	X		
Hamsters	X	X					
Snakes	X						
Lizards	X	X					

What is the total number of pets that this class has?

_____

Which pet has the lowest number?

_____

What was the amount?

_____

Which three pets have the same amounts?

_____

_____

_____

If you doubled the amount of cats, what number would you get?

_____

Would there still be more dogs based on this new number?

yes   no

How many pets are not dogs or cats?

_____

Which kind of pet was there the most of?

_____

How many more snakes are needed so that the number of snakes equals the number of dogs?

_____ snakes

Find the sum when you add the numbers of:

snakes + lizards +

dogs + fish = _____

List the kinds of pets in order from the most to the fewest.

Scholastic • Tic-Tac-Math: Grades K–2

Name(s): _____

Wildcat Basketball

Answer three problems to get Tic-Tac-Math!

WILDCAT BASKETBALL Points scored for each player:	Charlie	4
	Chris	7
	Bob	10
	Alex	6
	Jamie	12
	Aaron	2
	Ryan	10
	Andrew	14

Which person scored an odd number of points?

_____

What is the number of points?

_____

Write the points in order from lowest to highest.

(Don't write the players' names, just the points.)

Who scored the least number of points for the Wildcats?

_____

How many points did that player get?

_____

What is the difference between the highest points scored and the lowest points scored?

_____

Two people scored the same number of points. Who are they?

_____
_____

How many points did they score together?

_____

What is the total points scored?

_____

The Wildcats played against a team that scored 75. Did the Wildcats win?

yes   no

Who scored the most points for the Wildcats?

_____

How many points did that player get?

_____

How many players scored above 5 points?

_____

When added together, which two players' points total another player's points?

_____
_____

Can you find another combination?

Scholastic • Tic-Tac-Math: Grades K–2

Name(s): _____

At the Zoo

Answer three problems
to get Tic-Tac-Math!

ANIMALS WILLIE SAW AT THE ZOO			
Bears	12	Monkeys	24
Penguins	17	Lions	4
Gorillas	9	Elephants	5
Tigers	3	Hippos	6

Which animal did Willie see more of? Circle the correct answer.

    tigers or hippos

    bears or gorillas

monkeys or lions

penguins or bears

Which animal did Willie see the most of?

_____

How many of these did he see?

_____

Which three animals can you add together to get the total of another animal? Show your equation.

Willie saw more monkeys than gorillas. How many more monkeys did he see than gorillas?

_____

Use the data from the chart to make a bar graph on the back of this paper. Write the names of the animals across the bottom of the graph.

Find the sum when you add the numbers of:

gorillas + hippos + penguins = _____

What is the total number of animals Willie saw at the zoo?

_____

Double check your answer.

List the three groups of animals Willie saw the least of.

_____

_____

When Willie saw the monkeys, half of them were sleeping. How many were awake?

_____

Scholastic • *Tic-Tac-Math: Grades K–2*

Name(s): _____

Rising Temperatures

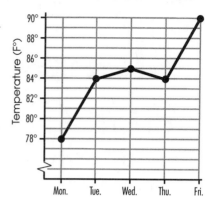

Use this line graph to answer three problems and get Tic-Tac-Math!

What does this graph show? _____ _____ _____ _____	**On what day was the temperature the highest?** _____ **What was the temperature?** _____	**On which day was the temperature 85°?** _____
On which two days was the temperature the same? _____ _____	**What was the temperature on Monday?** _____	**How many degrees warmer was Friday than Thursday?** _____
How many degrees cooler was Monday than Wednesday? _____	**On what day was the temperature the lowest?** _____ **What was the temperature?** _____	**On which day would you go to the beach? Why?** _____

Scholastic • Tic-Tac-Math: Grades K–2

Name(s): _____

Sleepy Bar Graph

Use this bar graph to answer three problems and get Tic-Tac-Math!

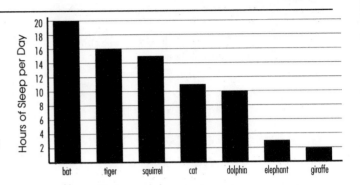

What does this graph show?

_____

_____

_____

_____

Which animal sleeps the most number of hours a day?

_____

How many hours?

_____

How many hours does a squirrel sleep in a day?

_____

Which sleeps more, a tiger or a squirrel?

_____

How many more hours does a bat sleep than a cat?

_____

Which animal sleeps the least number of hours a day?

_____

How many hours?

_____

How many animals sleep more than 10 hours a day?

_____

Which animal sleeps only 3 hours a day?

_____

How many hours do you sleep in a day?

_____

Add a bar on the graph showing how many hours. Label the bar with your name.

Name(s): _____

Mystery Number

Read the clues to figure out each Mystery Number. Write the Mystery Number in the box. Answer three problems to get Tic-Tac-Math!

- 2 groups of 4
- 1 more than 7
- 3 plus 5

- 1 ten and 2 ones
- 3 groups of 4
- 2 more than 10

- 6 less than 12
- 1 group of 6
- 3 plus 3

- 2 more than 15
- 1 less than 18
- 1 ten and 7 ones

- 7 plus 2
- 9 ones
- 1 more than 8

- 10 more than 1
- 9 plus 2 minus 0
- 11 less than 22

- 1 ten and 8 ones
- 6 groups of 3
- 9 doubled

- 3 more than 17
- 2 groups of 10
- 5 + 5 + 5 + 5

- 10 + 10 − 19
- 1 group of 1
- 9 less than 10

Name(s): _____

Mystery Number

Read the clues to figure out each Mystery Number.
Write the Mystery Number in the box. Answer three
problems to get Tic-Tac-Math!

- Less than 10
- Greater than 5
- An odd number
- 3 + 3 + 3

- Greater than 7
- Less than 15
- An even number
- 5 groups of 2

- An even number
- Greater than 10
- 1 is in the tens place
- 6 doubled

- 2 is in the tens place
- Greater than 20
- Less than 30
- 5 groups of 5

- An odd number
- Less than 10
- Greater than 4
- 3 + 2 + 2

- Less than 20
- Greater than 10
- An even number
- 9 doubled

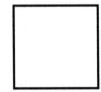

- An even number
- 6 is in the ones place
- Greater than 10
- Less than 20

- 5 is in the ones place
- Greater than 10
- Less than 30
- 5 groups of 3

- Greater than 20
- An even number
- 11 doubled
- 3 less than 25

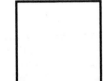

Name(s): _____

Mystery Number

Each box has four numbers. Read the clues to figure out which number is the Mystery Number. Circle the correct number.

6, 7, 8, 9, 10

---

45   25   10   53

- It is more than 20.
- It has a 5 in the ones place.
- It is less than 30.

81   50   23   45

- It is less than 60.
- It is an odd number.
- It has a 2 in the tens place.

62   31   18   20

- It is an even number.
- It is less than 24.
- It is 5 groups of 4.

---

84   102   408   48

- It is greater than 50.
- It has a 0 in it.
- When you add 100 to it, you get 202.

452   952   421   654

- It is greater than 450.
- It is an even number.
- It has a 5 in the tens place.
- It is greater than 950.

127   307   67   142

- It has a 7 in the ones place.
- It is greater than 100.
- It has a 0 in the tens place.

---

795   895   995   305

- It has a 5 in the ones place.
- It is an odd number.
- It is more than 500.
- It is 5 less than 1,000.

199   47   124   109

- It is greater than 100.
- It is an odd number.
- It is 1 less than 200.

429   381   364   533

- It has a 3 in it.
- It is an odd number.
- It is greater than 300.
- The numbers add up to 12.

Scholastic • Tic-Tac-Math: Grades K–2

Fun With the 100 Chart

Use the 100 chart (page 56) for the problems below. Complete three to get Tic-Tac-Math!

Color all numbers that end with a 0 red.	Color all numbers that end with a 5 yellow.	List five numbers that are less than 100 and have a 1 in the tens place.
Practice skip counting by 2's on the 100 Chart. Touch each number as you say it.	Color all numbers that end with a 1 blue.	Find all "twin" numbers, such as 22, 55, and so on. Circle these numbers.
Fill in the missing numbers from the 100 Chart.	List eight even numbers that are greater than 50.	With a friend, play "Race to 100" on the 100 Chart. Place two game markers (coin or button) on 1. Take turns rolling a number cube and moving that many spaces on the chart. The first player to reach 100 wins.

Fill in the missing numbers grid:

33		35
43		

List eight even numbers that are greater than 50:

_____ _____

_____ _____

_____ _____

_____ _____

Scholastic • *Tic-Tac-Math: Grades K–2*

Name(s): _____

100 Chart Challenge

Use the 100 chart (page 56) for the problems below. Complete three to get Tic-Tac-Math!

Fill in the missing numbers on the grid.

62		64	
	73		

Color all the even numbers that are greater than 50 green.

List all the numbers that have a 0 in the tens place.

Circle all the numbers that have a 5 in the ones place. If there was one more number under 95, what would that number be?

_____

Use the 100 Chart to solve these tricky math problems.

26 + 14 = _____

57 + 19 = _____

66 + 21 = _____

19 + 18 = _____

Color all the odd numbers that are less than 50 blue.

Fill in the missing numbers from the 100 Chart.

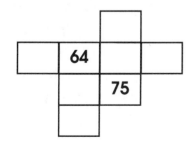

Fill in the missing numbers from this piece of the 100 Chart.

	58		60
	68	69	
77			

What number in the 100 Chart is:

• under number 10? _____

• above number 55? _____

• above number 91? _____

• under number 13? _____

• above number 49? _____

100 Chart

1	2	3	4	5	6	7	8	9	10
11	12	13	14	15	16	17	18	19	20
21	22	23	24	25	26	27	28	29	30
31	32	33	34	35	36	37	38	39	40
41	42	43	44	45	46	47	48	49	50
51	52	53	54	55	56	57	58	59	60
61	62	63	64	65	66	67	68	69	70
71	72	73	74	75	76	77	78	79	80
81	82	83	84	85	86	87	88	89	90
91	92	93	94	95	96	97	98	99	100

Scholastic • Tic-Tac-Math: Grades K–2

Name(s): _____

The Merry Month of March

Use the March calendar (page 59) with this Tic-Tac-Math sheet.

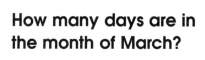

How many days are in the month of March? _____ days	On what day of the week does this month start? _____ On what day of the week does this month end? _____	How many days in this month are Mondays? _____ How many days in this month are Thursdays? _____
Color all of the odd-numbered days red. How many days did you color? _____	What day of the week will April 1st be? _____ What day of the week will April 8th be? _____	If today is March 19th, how many days are there until the end of the month? _____ days Write a math equation to show this. _____ _____ = _____
Write the dates for all the Wednesdays in this month.	Color all of the even-numbered days yellow. How many days did you color? _____	How many weekend days are there in this month? _____ Saturdays _____ Sundays _____ Total weekend days

Scholastic • Tic-Tac-Math: Grades K–2

Name(s): _____

See You in September

Use the September calendar (page 59) with this Tic-Tac-Math sheet.

Put an X through all the weekend days.

On how many days did you put an X?

_____

Write down the dates for all the Thursdays in this month.

Circle all of the even-numbered days on this calendar.

How many days did you circle?

_____

Find all the number 1's on this calendar. How many did you find? _____

Tell someone what each of the number 1's represent (for example, one tens, one ones, and so on).

If today is Monday, September 6th, how many days until Thursday, September 23rd?

_____ days

On what day of the week was August 29th?

_____

On what day of the week will October 2nd be?

_____

Sienna went on vacation for two weeks. She got home on September 26th.

On what date did she leave for vacation?

_____

Today is Tuesday, September 14th. I have an appointment in 8 days. What is the date of my appointment?

_____

1 week = _____ days

2 weeks = _____ days

3 weeks = _____ days

4 weeks = _____ days

Scholastic • *Tic-Tac-Math: Grades K–2*

March Calendar

Sunday	Monday	Tuesday	Wednesday	Thursday	Friday	Saturday
	1	2	3	4	5	6
7	8	9	10	11	12	13
14	15	16	17	18	19	20
21	22	23	24	25	26	27
28	29	30	31			

September Calendar

Sunday	Monday	Tuesday	Wednesday	Thursday	Friday	Saturday
			1	2	3	4
5	6	7	8	9	10	11
12	13	14	15	16	17	18
19	20	21	22	23	24	25
26	27	28	29	30		

Name(s): _____

Let's Review!

Answer three problems to get Tic-Tac-Math!

Finish these patterns:

A B B A ____ ____ ____

2, 5, 4, 7, 6, ____ ____ ____

99, 88, 77, ____ ____ ____

X X O O X ____ ____ ____

List 5 ways to make $1 using nickels, dimes, and quarters.

How many corners on:

5 triangles? _____

3 squares? _____

4 hexagons? _____

6 circles? _____

People are walking with their umbrellas open. What weather is most likely outside?

sunny   rainy   cloudy

---

9   5   2   8

Using these numbers, what is the largest number you can make?

_____

What fraction is the shaded part?

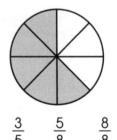

$\frac{3}{5}$ $\frac{5}{8}$ $\frac{8}{8}$

Read the clues to figure out the mystery number:

• It is an even number.

• It has a 3 in the tens place.

• It is 3 groups of 12.

What is the number?

_____

Today is Wednesday, February 8th. What will the day and date be 5 days from now?

_____

Marcia invited 4 friends for a play date. She plans to give each friend 3 stickers. How many stickers does she need in all?

_____

Answers

What's My Number? (page 9)

2, 5, 8, 10	Activity	40 10 100 16 17 101 90 (circled)
3 11 5 17	Activity	3 7 8
10 10	0, 1, 2, 3, 4, 5, 6, 7, 8, 9, 10	17 | 9 12 | 5 7 | 8

Number Sense (page 10)

Activity	4 | 3 2 | 11 1 | 7	6 9 12 14
5, 10, 15, 20, 25, etc.	4, 5, 6, 7, 8, 9, 10, 11, 12	Activity
1 6 3 4	15 95 5 105 525 65 (circled)	13, 14, 15, 16, 17, 18, 19

Getting to Know Numbers (page 11)

2 10 9 19	1 2 3 4	6 1 12 9
3 crayons	6, 8, 11, 13, 14, 16, 19	Activity
Answers will vary.	15, 14, 13, 12, 11, 10, 9, 8	Activity

Numbers Everywhere! (page 12)

5; 3	12, 14, 18, 20, 22, 24, 25	II IIII JHT II
7 8 9 10	3 — six 6 — seven 7 — two 2 — three	4 6 9 18 0
25	Activity	Answers will vary.

Missing Numbers (page 13)

Answers will vary.	28, 38, 58, 68, 88	6 5 4 3
even	6, 8, 10, 12, 14, 16, 18, 20	11, 13 19, 21 6, 8 35, 37
2 4 6 8	5 4 3 2	27 98 45

Writing Numbers (page 14)

JHT JHT JHT JHT JHT; JHT JHT JHT JHT JHT IIII; JHT JHT JHT III	15 | 20 88 | 17	12 14 16 18
1 2 3 4 5	20, 40, 50, 70, 80, 100, 120, 140	6 8 8 6 even
24, 34, 54, 74, 84, 114	Answers will vary.	Answers will vary.

Making Sense of Numbers (page 15)

Answers will vary.	7, 5, 39, 81, 87, 23	100, 103, 105, 107, 109
303	53 88 105 72	Answers will vary.
6 6 6 6	< > = <	15, 13, 11, 9, 7, 5

I've Got Your Number! (page 16)

425, 427, 428, 429, 431, 433	Activity	Answers will vary.
16 69 220 639	Answers will vary.	Answers will vary.
10 10 10 10 10	8 12 4 5	137 731

Numbers Get Bigger (page 17)

62 43 118 2,020	9 19 24 34	no
4 tens	20	Answers will vary.
326 539 172 250	3,827 3,836 3,926 4,826	2 8 99 10

What's in a Number? (page 18)

10	(shaded square)	7 straws
(dots: ● ● ○ / ● ● ● ● / ○ ○ ○ ○)	872	6 eyes
5 groups	1,562 1,085 4,920 2,471	15 246 5,932 908

Hurray for Patterns! (page 19)

x o A B 1 2 O o	Activity	Activity
Answers will vary.	Activity	○ □ ○
Answers will vary.	Answers will vary.	Answers will vary.

61

Do You See a Pattern? (page 20)

Activity	Answers will vary.	A B Z X H I
6 7 8 each number goes up by 1	Activity	Activity
2 1 3 1 2 1 2 1	oo oooo oo oooo oo	Activity

There's a Pattern Here! (page 21)

40; no	Activity	Activity
X x ↑ ↓ ○ oo	Activity	3 inches
yes no yes yes	1 block	Activity

Pretty Patterns! (page 22)

Activity	10 pounds	yes no yes yes yes
8, 10 12, 15 7, 9 7, 6	39, 49, 59, 69, 79, 89, 99, 109	
●● ● ○	Activity	Activity

Growing Patterns (page 23)

IIII, IHI, IHI I, IHI II, IHI III	Activity	2 + 2 = 4 2 + 1 = 3 1 + 2 = 3
his brother 2 years	oooooooooo	18, 20 35, 45 110, 120 404, 505
33 yes	400 500 600 700	Activity

Patterns to Bark About! (page 24)

12 legs	6 3 8 9 0	55 odd
9 times	4 + 1 = 1 + 4 1 + 3 = 3 + 1 5 + 0 = 4 + 1	50,000 70,000
16, 20 20, 25 93, 91 44, 55	6	12 points

Pick a Pattern (page 25)

XXXXXXXX	13, 17 37, 47 19, 22 16, 32	ABAB
7 16 35 20	6 legs	18
yes no no no	80 cents	8 18

Patterns Are Us! (page 26)

Activity	100	10; 60
46, 56, 66 no	6 6 1 20	$2.50
Answers will vary.	21 28 35	21 times

Finding Shapes! (page 27)

Activity	Answers will vary.	circle or oval
square	Answers will vary.	○ ○ ○ □ □ □
Activity	Activity	3 4 6 4

What's in a Shape? (page 28)

○ ○	5	△ ○ □
Answers will vary.	ATE	Activity
circle rectangle triangle		triangle (sail); rectangle (mast); trapezoid (boat)

Geometry (page 29)

○ ○ □ □ □ □	4 3 4 0	Activity
Activity		triangle
Answers will vary.	Activity	Activity

The Shape of Things (page 30)

Answers will vary.	Activity	circle
square		Activity
Answers will vary.	STOP	

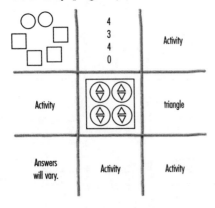

Shape Up! (page 31)

[dominoes]	Answers will vary.	[triangle]
triangle	Activity	[rock shapes]
4	Activity	yes no

Amazing Shapes! (page 32)

cylinder, sphere, cube, pyramid; cylinder and sphere can roll	Answers will vary.	Answers will vary.
top	[shape cards]	Activity
[dice]	Activity	Answers will vary.

Put It Together (page 33)

[star]	Activity	circle
[shape]	sphere cylinder rectangular prism	bottom
36 corners	Activity	pyramid

Not Just Shapes! (page 34)

14 squares	[triangle]	Activity
M	green	Answers will vary.
12 12 12	square	pentagon

Time for Measurement (page 35)

5 cents 10 cents	elephant car brick bike cat	Answers will vary.
Answers will vary.	[clock]	nickel
Answers will vary.	morning night	24¢

Weigh It! (page 36)

Activity	Answers will vary.	crayon bike mouse telephone pencil
Answers will vary.	Activity	70¢; 80¢
[clock]	dime	September, October, November, December

Money and More (page 37)

1 dollar 1 quarter 10 pennies 12 pennies	January, March, May, July, August, October, December	48¢
Answers will vary.	Activity	Saturday, Sunday
Activity	6:15	Friday Monday

Measure These! (page 38)

5¢ 25¢ 50¢ $1.25	3 cups 1 cup 1/2 cup 1 cup	Jack
Answers will vary.	3 pounds	Monday, November 10
[clock] 9:15	Answers will vary.	Answers will vary.

What's There to Measure? (page 39)

14 cans	21 degrees	Answers will vary.
Answers will vary.	30¢	[clock] 2:30
Monday	8 12 1/2	10¢ 50¢ $1.00 $2.50 $10.00

Measure Up! (page 40)

2 quarters 4 dimes 2 dollars 8 dimes 7 nickels	12 cm	a ruler a scale a cup
[clock]	2 quarters, 2 dimes, 2 pennies	Answers will vary.
summer	$702	24 36 6

Fun With Measurement (page 41)

$22	Answers will vary.	62°
14	39	6
15¢	2 minutes 1 hour 250 minutes 60 minutes	13 cm

Measure for Measure (page 42)

nickels	inches feet	7:00 A.M.
4 4 2	20 inches	36°F
Activity	$2.55	Activity

Make a Guess (page 43)

12 times	Answers will vary.	Activity
Answers will vary.	3 circles 2 squares	rain in the summer
Answers will vary.	1's = 3 3's = 4 2's = 4 4's = 3	Activity

Heads or Tails? (page 44)

Answers will vary.	Answers will vary.	2's = 6 1's = 3 4's = 2 3's = 1
Answers will vary.	Answers will vary.	Answers will vary.
You should have pulled more red blocks because there are more red blocks than blue.	4 circles 6 squares 10 shapes more squares	Answers will vary.

Colorful Candies (page 45)

28 candies	yellow orange	16 candies
3, 5, 8, 12	yellow and orange	5 more
5 − 3 = 2	25	yellow and red; 12 − 8 = 4

Our Pets (page 46)

24 pets	snakes 1	birds, hamsters, lizards
10 no	12	dogs
6	15	dogs; fish and cats; birds, hamsters, and lizards; snakes

Wildcat Basketball (page 47)

Chris 7 points	2, 4, 6, 7, 10, 10, 12, 14	Aaron 2 points
12	Bob and Ryan 20 points	65 points no
Andrew 14 points	6 players	Answers will vary, but should be one of these: Jamie + Aaron = Andrew; Charlie + Alex = Bob or Ryan; Bob or Ryan + Charlie = And; Aaron + Bob or Ryan = Jam

At the Zoo (page 48)

hippos bears monkeys penguins	monkeys 24	Answers will vary, but should be one of these: gorillas + tigers + elephants = penguins; bears + gorillas + tigers = monkeys; penguins + tigers + lions = monkeys
15 more monkeys	Activity	9 + 6 + 17 = 32
80 animals	tigers, lions, elephants	12 monkeys were awake

Rising Temperatures (page 49)

The temperature from Monday to Friday	Friday 90°	Wednesday
Tuesday and Thursday	78°	6° warmer
7° cooler	Monday 78°	Answers will vary.

Sleepy Bar Graph (page 50)

How many hours different animals sleep in a day	bat 20 hours	15 hours
tiger	9 more hours	giraffe 2 hours
4 animals	elephant	Answers will vary.

Mystery Number (page 51)

8	12	6
17	9	11
18	20	1

Mystery Number (page 52)

9	10	12
25	7	18
16	15	22